From Syria With Love

Voices of the Syrian Refugee Children

Molly Masters

From Syria With Love
Voices of the Syrian Refugee Children

Edited by Molly Masters

ISBN: 978-1-908041-34-0

Published by IndieBooks
4 Staple Inn, London, WC1V 7QH

www.indiebooks.co.uk

Set in Corbel 12/14

Printed by CPI, Durham, DH1 1TW

The proceeds of this book will go directly to the charity 'From Syria With Love' to support the children of the Al Abrar camp featured in this book, as well as others across Syria and Lebanon.

Contents

Foreword

The Syrian people have a tradition of providing a refuge to those in need: the Circassians in 1870, the Armenians in 1915, the Palestinians in 1948, and the Iraqis in 2003.

Now the Syrian people need our help. In five years of civil war, hundreds of thousands have been killed or injured, and many more have been forced to flee their homes. They need us to put pressure on governments and world leaders to bring about a lasting peace; and to provide aid and support to those who have been diasplaced by fighting.

And for our own sakes, as well as theirs, we must challenge the poisonous idea that refugees do not deserve our aid and our compassion, or that they pose some kind of threat to us.

As we approach another winter, with so many Syrians living in makeshift camps, the need for practical aid, raising funds for food, medicines and shelter, is paramount. But aid alone is not enough, if we allow prejudice to gain a hold.

This makes *From Syria with Love* so timely. The money it raises will go straight to help the children who are featured in its pages. But more than that, by seeing the world through these children's eyes, and hearing their voices, we are reaffirming our common humanity.

Caroline Lucas

Introduction

The idea behind the charity From Syria with Love is a simple one: to be a link between Syrian refugees and the world, primarily through taking pictures drawn by children living in a refugee camp in Lebanon and exhibiting them in Britain, to show the reality of their lives, and to raise funds to help improve their conditions and future prospects.

The exhibitons staged have shown the power of this idea. People around the country have responded with huge generosity. The exhibitions have opened people's eyes to the human consequences of the civil war in Syria.

This was my own experience. Before hearing about From Syria With Love, I felt so distanced from the Syrian crisis. I was passionate that something should be done; but helpless about what I personally could do. I didn't have a lot of money to spare as a first year university student, but I did have time. I saw an advert for the charity's exhibition in Brighton. There I absorbed the beautiful and tragic paintings, and through the stories they told, or hinted at, I learned more and more of the scale and effect of this crisis. I listened to a presentation by Baraa Ehssan Kouja, the charity's founder, absorbing more about Syria's rich and harmonious past, and about its destruction. I was intrigued as to how they were operating here in the UK, yet able to make such a difference all the way across the world in Lebanon. Despite the ominous tone of sadness in the air, I could finally feel a sense of hope. I decided to buy a painting as a unique memoir of the experience and selected the butterfly picture by Emad, who is six years old. When I saw it on the wall, my heart almost stopped. It was as if I was looking at my own framed painting from when I was the same age. I used to draw my butterflies in just the same way: big round wings with patterns dancing in the middle, and even bigger googly eyes. I remember my own eyes welling at the similarity: I'd never felt closer.

This led me to volunteer with the charity, and to propose a book to take the work of the charity to new audiences.

I didn't, at first, appreciate the challenges. Travel to the Al Abrar camp is impractical, so the work of collecting the stories of the children, to go alongside their pictures, has been done by video recordings and emails. Helping the children to tell their stories has needed a lot of care, particularly given the traumatic experiences that many have passed through. And there is also the challenge of translation: not only from Arabic to English, but also helping to shape the stories of the children, to help readers unfamiliar with the Arab world to engage more fully.

In the latter, I have been helped enormously by having creative voices who have lent their own talents to interpret, or be inspired by, the pictures and stories of the children of the Al Abrar camp. The enthusiasm with which the children have contributed to this book shows how important it is to them to know that, thousands of miles away, there are people who want to know about their lives – and who want to help.

Towards the start of the book, I have included one of the transcripts of the interviews we conducted; and towards the end, I have described as best I can one of the videos showing life in the camp. You will find more of these on the charity's website and on YouTube. Along with stories, poems, diaries, personal messages and even an exchange of letters between two pen pals – Poppy and Ghaithaa – brought togther by the exhibition, this book tries to capture something of the lives of the children in Al Abrar – their dreams, their memories, and their hope that, one day soon, they will be able to return to the country they love so much.

Above all, in their pictures and words, we have a unique window on their world; one that is an essential complement to the images of war and destruction that we see each day in the news; one which, I hope in time will prevail.

Molly Masters

The children of the Al Abrar refugee camp.

Listen to the Children

Half the world's refugees are children - around eight million of them.

The number is so shocking that we can't help longing for a single, huge answer to the situation. And it's right that we should do that. It's important to confront and tackle the huge global issues that drive millions of children from their homes every year.

But looking for huge solutions isn't enough. If that's all we do, we're in danger of seeing the refugees themselves as 'problems'. And that's not true. The problems are wars and famines and disasters.

The refugees are people.

That's why it's important to keep remembering that each of those children - every single one - is an individual, with different likes and dislikes, different fears and failings and a unique set of abilities. Given the chance, they can enrich the world in millions of different ways.

It's not easy to grasp that when the numbers are so huge. But there is one very simple thing we can do to keep it in our minds.

We can listen to the children themselves.

Gillian Cross

'When I Think of Syria...'

I think it was very happy, but now...

I can feel it calling me. I used to feel like we had to stay in it, then we fled, but now we have to go back.

When I hear its beautiful name. I used to think it was beautiful before the war.

...I think of when my grandparents used to talk to me, and tell me that: 'Syria is fine, the route to Syria is opened again' – and I used to be so happy.

...I feel that Syria is calling us to stand beside it. Now it is waiting for us to return.

...I think of when the siege happened, and we saw it calling us, it wanted us, but we didn't reply, we wanted to reply.

When I think of Syria, now, I know its name belongs in the past, because Syria is gone now, and we have no chance to return.

...I feel it telling each Syrian 'may God never forgive you'.

When I think of Syria, I think of how I never used to think of Syria when I was in it. I never thought I will miss it, but now, most of my misses are for Syria.

An Interview

Q: Who would like to answer the first question?

Kawthar: Me.

Q: How was your life before the war, Kawthar?

Kawthar: It was beautiful, so much more than now.

Q: Shall we go by turns or go to Majd?

All: Majd.

Majd: We were living in houses, and now we are living in camps.

Tasneem: It was so much more beautiful, now we are in camps, before we were in palaces.

Douha: No, for me now is more beautiful, because I started to achieve what I want, and the ones who says before it was more beautiful, it's because they don't want to run after their ideas and dreams.

Nada: Come back to me later.

Nour: It was more beautiful before because we were living in houses, and in our country, but here we are displaced, and no longer like one family, each one is living by themselves.

Abdo: Here we are not happy, but in Syria it was better.

Mousa: We were all happy and together and now each one is apart.

Emad: No comment.

Nada: We were living in palaces, now in camps our life is not beautiful, as Douha said we came here to run after our ideas, but we still want to go back to our country.

Nour: It was beautiful, we used to give examples of people living in tents for the not happy life.

Q: How was your life before the war?

Kawthar: It was so good, now I started to chase my dream, I have registered in photography workshop.

Q: What is the best memory in your life:

Kawthar: Later.

Tasneem: Later.

Douha: Best memory in my life will be after the war ends in Syria, that I have met my friends here, especially Aya and Tasneem.

Nour: The memory is not now, is later when I become proud of my self after being Arabic teacher.

Bayan: Best memory was when I used to play with my friends at school (laughter) but now my friend is gone.

Tasneem: When dad was here, and we used to gather all of us, we have never thought we will be separated one day, but now it happened and we are.

Kawthar: Best memory in my life the month of Ramadan before the Syrian crisis, that was my best memory.

Q: How do you spend your day in the camp, what is life to you?

Kawthar: I don't spend too much time in the camp, living in the camp doesn't change my life if I live in a tent or not, I go to workshops, go out and take pictures outside, and play here with the children.

Tasneem: I spend my day with Douha, we play together, draw together, study together, we spend most of our times together, we don't like to separate from each other.

Douha: I spend all my day with Aya and Tasneem.

Nour: I spend all day with my friend Sally from school, sometimes we fight with each other, but we talk with each other again after.

The children performing at a camp event.

نار

صبوا علينا نار

مات الزعتر, خطي معتر

وتغطى صابون الغار

جار الزمن علينا يا جار

والموت غلبنا

الهاشتاق صار رسمالك يا حلبنا

ما تزيد وتعيد وتقلي بكرا بتعمر الدار

ما ينسى والله الي يدمر

كبر بالله وزيف دينك وحور

غير اسلامك ليصير الحال

حدا على قلعة على نخلة بكي حداد

على صغير ياما شجع الاتحاد

ولاد ربيو اخوة

كبروا باسم النخوة قتلوا بعض

طاب تراب الوطن عن الدفن

وتاجر البلد والتراب مات طعن

انا ما عم اقصد حدا

They poured us with fire. Thyme and soap are so dusty, The time passed, and death defeated us. They supported Aleppo with a hash tag, and told us they would rebuild it again. Don't say you will build it while you destroy it and change its religion.Children were friends, then became enemies. And the soil of our country was sold pricelessly. I don't mean anybody, I mean everybody. When a person cries in Aleppo, the sound is heard in Damascus. You, O Senator, who walks proudly and mocks the dead bodies.

Listen to the Children

انا عم اقصد كل حدا

والصوت لما يأن بحلب

تسمع بالشام الصدى

يا شيخ ياللي بمجلس الشعب تمختر

وعلى جثثك يا شعب يا درويش تمسخر

يا شيخ ياللي سما الاطفال كبب ومشاوي

يا حيوان لولا حلب الشهباء شو ايدك بتساوي

ويللي ناوي بمجلس الامن يتدخل

ويفك النعش

متل الي غاوي تنفك هلارض

انسى

لك يا عمي انسى الكل عم ينسى

انسى نشوة عسكري للمستقبل بالتسريح

انسى نشوة مغترب اخده الموج والريح

انسى نشوة مواطن ضايع بين التكفير والتشبيح

انسى يا خاين, انسى الغرب والعرب

واحضن قذيفتك وارقص على رصاصتك والضرب

ما تصدق انو الحب متل الحرب

وانو بدا زلم

الحب متل حلب شبعان ظلم

For those who say the Security Council would interfere in Syria, how could the case be solved by the Monster. Don't forget how the soldiers hope to finish their military service and get back home. Never think that love is similar to war. Love is as Aleppo. Both are full of iniquity.

This poem was written by Douha and performed at the Al Abrar camp's Eid celebration.

Kawthar

My name is Kawthar. I am 17 years old.

I am a Syrian refugee living in Lebanon camp, and I escaped from Homs with my family two and a half years ago. Our living conditions are so hard. I live in a tent with my mother and my six sisters.

When I came from Syria my life stopped, everything has changed; no education, no friends, no income since my father left us and remarried in Homs. Because of these conditions, we had to make something to live or to survive.

My mother was working until she was completely exhausted, and since I am the biggest sister I felt that maybe I can make something.

In our society, when a man wants to marry, it is the parent's responsibility to find the girl for their son, so this is exactly what happened. Two years ago, a woman and her daughter in our camp came to our tent and saw me, and then they said: 'we want you for our son'. It is very common to hear that. I didn't know the man before, but I was thinking 'They said he is 25 years old and he will give my family money', so I said yes I will marry him.

After that I got engaged for several months and I saw him just one time, the next time was in the wedding. I discovered that he is 28 years old. He does not know how to read and write. To be honest, I didn't like him at all, I didn't feel those feelings about love, passion, or even know him at all, but I couldn't stop or say anything while the time was passing, and I just I saw myself in the wedding dress with very bad feelings.

After the wedding we went to his tent, but I couldn't let him approach me, I don't know why but I was scared. At that time, he began to beat me severely and then went to sleep.

We continued in this situation for three days, and after that all his family started to beat me very badly.

I wanted to go to my family or escape, but they didn't let me until I had to lie and said 'I was raped before, please leave me alone', but they didn't believe me and they took me to a doctor who examined me and said I was a virgin.

We came back to his tent and before entering his sister attacked me and tore all my clothes, she pulled me inside and grabbed me tightly so my husband raped me.

After this I was crying all the time and I tried to kill myself several times. In the end, they took me to my family. My uncle was against me and he beat me two times, but my mother supported me and then we asked for a divorce.

After one month I got divorced, and I can tell you at that moment I was the happiest girl on this earth.

Now I don't think about any relationship any more, I think it is enough for me. But on the other hand, recently I saw a psychiatrist, and she is helping me to get through this and also I am taking a photography course, and I will make a gallery.

You know I couldn't see this before; there are many ways to live. You can study, work, and get money comfortably. Maybe this experiment was necessary to improve my life. Now I am planning to travel and take photos around the world. It was not the end; it was just a start, a real start.

Douha's Diary l

My name is Douha.

I will write what I used to do everyday. In general, I am in love with sleeping. In summer time I didn't used to wake up unless someone else has started to scream beside me.

I also used to do a drawing course, and on the course days I'd wake up at eight o'clock in the morning, and call my friend Aya, and then we would start to make some plans about how we would play some pranks. My other friend Tasneem used to come round with Aya and then we would go to the course. At two o'clock in the afternoon, we would finish and go back home, and I would show my paintings to my mum and then I'd have my lunch whilst I was watching an Indian movie. I really like them.

Sometimes me, Aya, Tasneem and Bayan would practice a Zumba dance, which is a Brazilian dance I know. Other times, I used to draw our bird. It was a very lovely bird and I cared about it a lot. I didn't like doing housework, like doing the dishes, and I always tried to escape from it or instead go and buy groceries that we needed to get out of it. At night, I used to be very quiet so that I could sleep. Me and sleeping are a love story, and my mum would destroy our love every morning.

This was my normal life.

The Pond

I don't spend too much time in the camp. Living in the camp doesn't change my life, if I live in a tent or not, I go to workshops, go out and take pictures outside, and play here with the children.

People probably think that living in this camp leaves us all stagnant, like weeds floating on top of a pond. For some, yes, this camp is a stagnant pond, a no-place, no-where, no-hope kind of pond. It's very easy to open the tarpaulin front of the tent in the morning, to look out on to the rubble and dust below one's feet and the darkening clouds in the sky and feel empty. You feel lifeless sometimes. But for some, like me, although it's not ideal, it's not what I wanted, this place is a place of opportunity. The stagnant pond isn't so stagnant all the time. There are children flitting around like little tadpoles, screaming and playing and learning and growing right before your eyes. There are families, collecting like lily pads, sticking together. There are teachers here, watching over us like tall, swaying grass, and food distributors swimming the surface like water striders. For me, living in the camp doesn't change or affect my life, whether I live in a tent or not. I am blessed to wake up every morning with my mother and sisters surrounding me, supporting me, and encouraging me. My mother, she is my strength, as she is to everyone in the camp. She is everyone's 'Auntie Rodeh' and I've never minded sharing her with all the other children. She walks outside of the tent and everyone adores her, she is like the sun gleaming over our pond, and everyone is basking in her glorious words and thriving in her loving embrace.

I can step outside the tent and see past the dust and clouds. I can breathe deeply, with widened nostrils, and smell something sweeter in the air. I feel privileged to be able to do this. It's as though I have a secret looking glass that no one else has, and I can see the future in the reflection of our pond, or I can see what is going to happen to us. When I think about it all, I know that God is looking after us, and that the future is brighter for us. My mother tells me, and all the children, the same. We are united in our knowledge of this.

I can step outside the tent fully, close the door behind me as not to disturb my sisters, and begin another day of opportunity. People probably assume there is no opportunity here, that we just await our aid and food and that is it, like a stagnant pond again. In my eyes, there is boundless opportunity here. If you have been here as long as me, and the other children, you will see that our eyes now glitter with the enthusiasm and thirst for opportunity. Your eyes have to glitter; otherwise you risk losing your spark. So, every day I do three things: I go to my workshops, I go and take pictures in the camp, and I play with the children. Taking pictures gives me a new sense of life, it allows me to use my looking glass eye and see myself being a photographer or a filmmaker in the future. I walk across the camp, past the same families and tents I have passed for many years; past the mothers feeding young children at the openings of their tents, inhaling the fresher air, past the fathers teaching trades to sons, past children teaching children. I smile politely at them all; we are all bonded as a family here.

My workshops take place in a small-bricked building with a tarpaulin roof. It is the living image of the word 'makeshift'. I duck my head to come in, and sit at one of the desks as the teacher discusses something with a child at the front. The children's eager voices always have and always will echo and bounce through the room, an excited energy that is completely contagious. The teacher begins to talk and a silence falls, it always does. Her words are all we have. We learn without books, and much of the time without pens and paper to ourselves. We share everything, especially our knowledge. When lessons are taught here, it's like skimming a stone across water. You can see those lessons ricocheting and vibrating through the children of the camp as one teaches another, one explains to the other, and they learn together. It's a ripple effect on the surface of our pond, it skims across everyone and enhances the future for us all.

The children have to be encouraged out of the school tent. Their feet move slowly and kick up dust on their way out. We thank our teacher in a chorus and make our way back to the hubbub of the camp. I run to catch up with our teacher, who leaves with a small bundle of papers under her arm.

'Can I use the camera today?' I ask, tapping her on the arm, as I do most days.

She turns and smiles as her eyes meet mine.

'Of course, Kawthar,' she takes it out of her satchel as she speaks, 'but please do bring it back in about an hour, in time for the photography workshop.'

'I will do, I promise!' I nod, my eyes fixated on the camera she extends towards me. This is my real looking glass. She taps me on the arm as I did for her, and continues on her way.

Looking through the lens, I can see the camp how I want to see it. I can take pictures of happiness, hope, and determination. I can take pictures of children playing with their friends amongst the grass, the bright colours reflecting the vibrancy of their expressions. I can take pictures of the aid being delivered, the children teaching each other, capturing the joy involved in our learning and sharing. I can take pictures of the faces of my friends as they learn new things in our classroom home. I can capture the camp as I see it, not as the world sees it. It's true, no one that is here wants to be here forever. But I am certain that a positive and hopeful attitude will reap positive results, and the more we can make the best of our situation here, through learning, sharing and acting, we can make progress for our own sake and the sake of Syria's future.

After returning my looking glass camera to the teacher, I take the walk back to my family's tents, stopping to see my friends and the other children as I pass. They are playing with rubber balls and small toys in an open square space of the camp. Some play catch, shouting and cheering and whooping at each other with every pass and catch. Some sing together. I know they have recently formed a band, the four of them, and they are sat in a huddle singing and harmonising. Others chase and tag, making whirlpools of rocks and dust as they skid and run. As the oldest child in the camp, I often feel too old for these games. It's all too easy to feel distanced from children as you grow, and start to focus more on what's ahead than what's happening now. So most days

I like to join in; to laugh like them, to play like them, and to feel like them. I sometimes feel like I am five years old, due to how much these past five years of the conflict have taught me. So many days I feel completely on their level, a level at which it must be so hard to comprehend and keep up with what is happening. Through all of my thoughts and onlooking, they continue to kick up dust and sing their songs. And so I join in.

People are too quick to assume that because we have nothing, we are nothing. But as long as we have our active minds, loving souls, and united spirits, we will always be stronger than the forces that oppose us. Life in our pond is forever stronger than the algae and winds of circumstance that may threaten it.

Kawthar Khalil with Molly Masters

Syria's
Children

Five years ago, Syria's children were safe, well fed, healthy, in education and living with their families. A child born since then has known almost nothing but war, insecurity, want and fear. Some 100 to 150,000 Syrian children have died. 2.6 million are out of school. Over 2 million are refugees, most of them in Jordan, Lebanon, Turkey and Egypt.

Eight thousand have travelled, unaccompanied, in search of safety. Many of those trapped inside Syria live in makeshift shelters, without warm clothing or enough food. As of now, the UK and other developed countries have resettled less than 2 percent of Syrians in need. Pledges to take more are not being honoured.

These facts shame us all.

Caroline Moorehead

Fond Memories

The following quotations are from the parents living in the Al Abrar camp in Lebanon.

'I have been here in Lebanon since 2013. I had three children, but after I met Douha, Aya, and Majd, they became six children. I want to say to the coming generations: be strong, be helpful like the children in the camp, the hope has just started, trust in yourself and you will be successful. I wish all the luck to you.'

'My son Emad's first word was 'mum', and the happiest memory I hold is when he started to walk. My son Emad always remembers his grandma and their picnics. He misses the family and safety.'

'My daughter Aisha's first word was 'mum' and the best memory I hold is when her brother Wael came. She misses home; life is in a house, not a tent.'

'My daughter Kawthar, she was a very cute girl. She used to laugh loudly. Her first word was 'bye'. The best memory I hold with her is when she went to the beach. Her sister Douha's first word was 'grandma'. She was a very smart girl; I remember our best memory was when she stashed her cousin between the blankets to stay together. The best memory for me with my children was every time we went to my parent's home and sat together. Douha always says: 'I miss my life in Syria, just in Syria'. Kawthar says it is enough that we once lived in Homs. And for me, it is enough that we learned what emigration means.'

'My son Mohammed's first word was 'father'. The best memory I hold was when he started to go to school and he was always singing. We were good before the war.'

'What have your parents taught you?'

To help the needy, and look after children and orphans.

To be strong when I encounter anything. They helped me with many things, they put me in school, and now I can read and write.

To be strong and tough, to not be scared of the bombings.

To help people sort out misunderstandings, and they gave me an education in school.

They taught me and helped with school work.

They taught me to help when I see someone in need, like an old lady who can't walk or needs help with a task. They are teaching me English so I can build my future.

'What will you teach your children?'

To endure, and to read the Quran.

To help people like themselves.

To love people and help them.

To endure, and to count on themselves.

To be like Auntie Rodeh.

To pray and read the Quran.

To draw.

Refugees

They have no need of our help
So do not tell me
These haggard faces could belong to you or me
Should life have dealt a different hand
We need to see them for who they really are
Chancers and scroungers
Layabouts and loungers
With bombs up their sleeves
Cut-throats and thieves
They are not
Welcome here
We should make them
Go back to where they came from
They cannot
Share our food
Share our homes
Share our countries
Instead let us
Build a wall to keep them out
It is not okay to say
These are people just like us
A place should only belong to those who are born there
Do not be so stupid to think that
The world can be looked at another way

(Now read from bottom to top.)

Brian Bilston

Snow

In the harsh winter of 2013, many Syrian refugees froze to death, eight of whom were children.

The children play. The clouds tiptoe.

The children gaze up. The clouds freeze. They continue to play.

The clouds extend their long white fingers and tickle the chins of the children. They laugh. Pure, white, innocent laughter.

The white flakes fall and the children reach tall. They catch them on their noses, their eyelashes, their elbows and their toes.

The long white hands reach and guide the children to their beds. Their bare feet crunch on the undisturbed blanket below. The flakes frost their hair, and turn their clothes to white. The children laugh, the clouds they smile, and then they bid goodnight.

The mothers they prattle and tuck them in blankets. The clouds they battle and tighten their grip. They cannot, they will not let the infants slip. The mothers they kiss the cold, white heads, and shed glassy tears when the clouds have fled. Their infants lie still in a pure cloud of white. They did not bid farewell before their final flight.

Molly Masters

Bloodstream

Like all five year olds, Emran is curious. Do dead children sink or float? Would he sink or float? His mother clutches him against the rucksack that she's heaved off her back and pushes him onto the deck of the wooden blue fishing trawler. The smell of snapper is overwhelming.

Behind her there's a commotion. A muharreb – people smuggler – has pulled out his kalashnikov and some of the women start wailing. One of the mothers still on land starts to plead with him. He's ripped open the top of her bag and pulled out a small machine with a little window on it.

– Tracking device, he screams in Arabic, but with a strange smooth, clipped and shaved accent.

– No, no, no! The father is trying to explain something. He's pointing at the machine and nodding and trying to smile in the way Emran's teacher smiles when it doesn't matter he's got something wrong.

The muharreb with the gun isn't calming down though. He's going through the bag again and screaming at them. The barrel of the gun is forced into the father's back and his wife slowly crumples to the ground.

– Get up woman.

Another muharreb pulls her up and she's stretching to get the bag but Emran can see the man's leg swing into the air and the bag is kicked into the sea. Emran pushes his face into his mother's skirt. He doesn't like watching grown-ups fight. And the couple are refusing to board, while the muharribeen are saying they will use their guns if they have to. They should shoot them here and now, but just get on the boat. Everyone has to get on the boat. Emran tightens his grip on his teddy.

– What's a tracking device, mami?

His mother is shaking. Shaking her head, shaking her hands – her whole body is shaking.

– Ssshhh Emran. It's not a tracking device.

– But why do they say it is?

– Ssshhh.

She pushes her son further along the boat towards the narrow entrance of the hull. Some people are trying in vain to turn back to see what's happening. He can just about hear the father.

– She'll die, she'll die, he's sobbing.

This makes Emran cry too because the last time he saw his own father, he was sobbing like that.

– Leave me baba! screams the daughter of the couple. Leave me here!

Emran knows the girl. It's Raghad and she's nice. She was in his sister's class at school. That was a long time ago but she would be thirteen like his sister.

– Who will look after Raghad if they go on the boat without her? asks Emran. He tries to thread his tiny fingers through his mother's. But he can't make a sailor's knot and he starts to cry.

– Mami.

– You'll be fine honey, she says, and smooths his salty hair.

But they're being pushed deeper into the hot hull; the families keep coming, people shout, move down keep moving down you at the back move down, and the families keep moving down, people keep shouting, he keeps moving down. Then the door of the hull is closed from the outside and the shouting stops. They listen to someone give instructions about steering: it's very simple, and see this red button and don't turn too suddenly.

Emran closes his eyes.

When he wakes, the sad family are opposite him. The mother is holding Raghad who is in a deep, deep sleep.

ೞ

Two days at sea and Emran wakes to crying and screaming: another fight. Raghad's mother is staring like she's playing a party game and the first one to blink is out. The father is at the front of the boat with the muharribeen. Then someone says something that sends a tremor through the human cargo. Italy doesn't take dead bodies. Emran's sure that's what he heard, but his mother is whispering to Raghad's mother and rocking her in her arms, so he can't ask.

Everyone is crying now.

– Where's Raghad? he quietly asks his mother later. He can't see the daughter.

– Al bahr ghaddar, she mutters. The sea is a betrayer.

Emran looks out across the cruel Mediterranean; the sea whose name Emran used to dread hearing back home. He'd heard about his cousin and like the other children, he'd used to pray that the rest of his family wouldn't be following the others. A bird on its way back from Africa swoops into the crest of a wave.

– Will Raghad sink or float, mami?

Kathryn Aldridge-Morris

Based on the true story of Raghad Hasoun, a thirteen year old Syrian girl who died after her diabetic machine and insulin were thrown into the sea by people smugglers, whom the family had paid with their last 1500 euros of savings. This was first published in Paris Lit Up *magazine in October 2016.*

Syrian

Walk across the street to go and collect the bread bundles to feed yourself and your family. Don't walk across the street. Don't walk anywhere. There are bombs and bullets that will take your life without warning. Don't walk; they're hiding in the alleyways. Turn on the tap, pour yourself a drink. Turn on the light, it's getting dark. Fill up the car with petrol. Or perhaps not. Go and fulfil your role as a man of your age, you've been called up. Don't. You'll be killed. You'll have to kill others. Try to flee, try to find an education, try to find a career. There's got to be another way. They will think you've come to preach your religion and fight the West. They will learn you've come to provide, they will. Use your savings; it's all you've got. The currency is falling, everything is expensive, just try to use your savings, you'll get by. You have no income or job. The savings should last you a while longer. Push it to the back of your mind. Don't look at the rubble around you. Don't listen to the noise. Don't inhale the dust that stagnates the air. You're in a warzone now, but there must be a future ahead, a new venture for you. Follow that hope. Follow the footsteps. Follow to somewhere safe. A promising horizon. When you get there, they'll stare. They might call you names, say something in the street. It's called discrimination, although no one will admit to it. You'll face it because of your race, your nationality, your religion, your country – just for being you. These people are brainwashed, understand that. They think you're a danger, and they're told you're not welcome. They can't see that you're just as horrified as they are about the state of the world. They just blame you for it. Try to do something. Get back on your feet. Get a job, perhaps. If you do, you'll get money and be able to provide again, food and water on the table. If you do, you'll be stealing jobs. If you don't, you'll starve. If you don't, you'll be living on benefits, stealing their money, in their eyes, that's what you came to do all along. Just when you feel like you can't take it anymore, it's exhausting every bone in your body, like it's a feeling made of lead, you think of going back. If you go back, you'll be killed. It's not like it was before. You dream of going back, but it's not like it was before. You'll still be an object, a label. Tarnished with one brush, part of a stereotype with everyone else. People won't see beyond the label you've been given. They won't see your personality, your determination, your love. They won't think about your struggle, your past, your trauma. They won't think how you wake at night, sweating and struggling after dreaming of what happened. They won't even consider that you might have anxiety, perhaps depression, that you need a kind word or even some help. They won't think about how difficult it is to learn their language, understand their culture, to try to immerse yourself in it. They won't even think about how you can't get a job, it's not allowed, not until you have your legal papers sorted, which will happen who knows when, and not until you have learned the language. They won't think about that.

They just won't think.

Baraa Kouja with Molly Masters

'What do you say to the countries that hosted or do not host refugees?'

Aya: To the countries who hosted, thank you, but I only say it as a compliment because some of them hosted us and used us. And for the ones who didn't host us, I would say you will need Syria one day.

Majd: I thank Syria because it hosted Palestinians before any other country. And for the countries which haven't hosted us, I am not surprised, they let Palestine down already.

Douha: I say to Arab countries specifically, I hate the song which says: 'Arab countries are my lands', rather it should be 'prepare the tents'. And I tell the foreign countries which hosted us: why do you take Syrian ID cards from us? And for the ones who haven't hosted us, I would say: what goes around comes around.

Tasneem: Thank you for hosting us when shelling and bombing were destroying our country. And to ones who haven't hosted us, when you need Syria one day, come. Syria doesn't close its doors to anyone.

Kawthar: For countries that hosted us: you made us live in tents. When Syria is healed and you come to visit, we will open our houses for you. And for countries that haven't hosted us, the days will prove for you that we don't need you, we can rebuild Syria again.

Mousa: I thank them because they hosted us. And for the ones who haven't hosted us, let them do whatever they want to do.

Mohammed: I thank Lebanon only, because I go to school there, and for countries who didn't host us, I say: we have God to look after us.

Ghaithaa: I didn't want to leave my home in the first place and I don't want to thank anyone.

The Doves of Syria

Vast, complete blue,
caressed by white,
embracing together,
Heaven and Earth,
as if on an artist's canvas.
Doves.
They glide,
purity and peace on beauty's wings.
Feather's kissed by the sun's gold,
loved by the sea of blue.
Below.
Their loving eyes can hardly
look.
Below.
The colourless mountains,
of rubble and soot,
colourless towers,
where they once stood.
Branches.
In their beaks they hold.
Branches of peace
  of healing
   of hope.
Their beaks release,
the branches fall down
  down
  down.
They float to the floor.

A nest,
It builds,
atop the rubble and soot,
colours of green and gold,
love underfoot.
Down.
The doves descend,
and land on human feet.
Safe in the nest,
they sing and speak,
their human hands busy,
they clear the debris,
a new world of Syria,
for all to see.
Doves may fly,
branches may fall,
but the children of Syria,
will restore hope to all.

Every Child
has the
Right to Dream

Kawthar slept...

...her lids fluttered like the quick opening and closing shutter of a camera lens. She stood from her crouched position, secured the camera around her neck once again, and brushed the dust from her knees. She coughed into her hand. The glove, too, was covered in dust.

'Okay, everyone!' she called, cupping her hands around her mouth to amplify her voice. The team were busy scrambling around the building they faced, overturning rubble, tables, beds, and brushing off dusty metal signs.

'Let's gather, please!' She ushered them over with her hand. The men and women made pools of rippling dust as they jumped down from heights and crawled out of the rubble on all fours. They carried film cameras on their shoulders, microphones under their arms, and smaller cameras around their necks like she did.

'What's next?' A woman a little shorter than Kawthar asked. She was wearing a pair of safety goggles, as she had been rummaging under some old school desks and amongst dangerous debris.

'I'd like some good panoramic shots of the sides of the building, some low angles near the bottom of it over there. Anas, Maya, can I leave that to you two?'

They nodded in response and formed their own small huddle to set up their tripods and lenses.

'If I could ask Hanan and Fathi to work on the interior shots of the building, I will come with you, and that leaves Layal and Ahmed to stay on the ground here with the radios. Make sure everyone can be seen, if not heard. Perhaps you'd like to do some sound recording of the rubble underfoot?'

'How shall we contact you when you're inside?' Ahmed reached for his radio clipped to his jacket.

'Let's use channel 7 for this one. I don't want to confuse it with any of the others!' She replied, spinning the dial on her own radio. She fastened the zip on her gilet, picked up her backpack of equipment, and gave a nod to Ahmed and Layal.

'Great work everyone!' She shouted with a broad smile as she, Hanan, and Fathi began to climb an exposed stairway with half an iron rail attached.

'I'll climb to the top and secure the ropes.' Hanan offered, passing them both on the staircase with nimble legs. She threw down a bundle of ropes resting on her shoulder and began to fasten them to the remaining part of the iron rail.

'Test it, Hanan, is it safe?' She called, hoisting her backpack higher onto her back. A leg of a tripod or something seemed to be digging into her spine.

'Totally safe, Kawthar.' Hanan laughed towards the end of her sentence. 'You alright there?'

She laughed and pulled her backpack up higher on her back.

'I'm fine!'

They reached the top of the staircase with their equipment and sighed as they laid it down on the floor. She stretched her back and heard it click in response, Hanan laughed again as she continued to tie up the ropes and clip the harnesses in place.

She looked around her. The broken staircase had lead them to a bricked room, scraps of wallpaper clung to the walls, and smashed glass littered the floor. There was a sturdy wooden door on the other side, the hinges still intact and the handle swinging loosely in the breeze coming through the hollowed-out window.

'Here we go, ready!' Hanan announced holding out the first harness and clip to her. She took it eagerly in her dusty gloved hands and started to attach herself. Hanan and Fathi did the same.

'Who wants to go first?' Fathi asked, adjusting the lock on his harness.

'I will,' she announced. 'I'll make sure the ground is steady and we can go ahead. There's a big risk with all this heavy equipment, and if we fall and lose it or it breaks, the documentary is over too. I know that won't happen. We have a great team here. But I'll go ahead first, just in case.'

She picked up her backpack from the floor, wriggled it around on her back to avoid the protruding tripod leg, and started towards the wooden door. She firmly grasped the handle; its metal was slightly hot after being exposed to the line of sunshine that fell on it. She pushed it down and pulled it towards her. Her eyes fluttered. Was it dust? Was it water? Something heavy was making her eyes squint, but she couldn't feel anything on her face, or on her body. She was walking, she knew that, but were her feet touching ground? Was she still on the harness? She tried to force her eyes open, her head felt dizzy, her body like a gust of wind, being pulled this way and that.

A thud. Her foot, hard concrete. Music, calling, shouting, laughing. Her ears, she could hear people. Spices, vegetables, cigarettes, rice, flowers, exhaust fumes. Her nose, it sang with the smell of food and life. Her eyes began to flutter, and she let go of the door handle and widened her eyes at the world before her.

Bustling, busier than ever before. She stepped into the street. People passed by, pushing this way and that. They carried baskets, babies, newspapers, bread, bicycles, mobile phones, leaflets, coffee, bags. A beep interrupted her awe, and she stepped onto the pavement out of the way of a passing car. It carried a family. Two children sat in the back, singing along to the loud radio. Above, people were pegging up their washing to dry on large lines on their balconies. The sky was bluer than blue, bluer than the water pouring from the central fountain on the roundabout ahead. Couples sat outside cafes, enjoying lunch and the sunshine overhead. Shopkeepers sold their fruit outside their shops from neat baskets and rows of crates. Children ran and played with backpacks on their back, books in their hands.

Her eyes brimmed, and she couldn't catch the tear rolling down her cheek.

'Can I help you,' a woman touched her arm and looked up at her face. 'You look lost?'

'No, no, thank you,' she nodded and smiled, touching the woman's hand affectionately. 'I'm home.'...

... Kawthar woke in a tent.

ം

Ghaithaa slept...

... He held his head in his hands. His shoulders were shrugging with every breath but he would not lift his head.

'Father, father, look at me.' She stood in front of him. Even stood at her full height, she was only just a little taller than where his head was resting. She touched his temples with her small hands.

'Baba,' she softened her voice. He looked up a little, enough to see her mouth perhaps. 'It's going to be ok. You have to try, you have to be determined.'

'My child,' he raised his head fully and his cheeks were red and his eyes tired. 'It is not going to work. I'm not strong enough.'

She turned to see the expression of her mother and the doctor across the room. They were the same. A mix of hopelessness and hopefulness. The burden seemed to lay on her words.

'Baba, please. You are strong enough, in your heart.

It is going to take time, but it will be worth it in the end. You have to try, please. For me, for Mohammed.'

Her brother stood next to his mother, his brow furrowed.

She held out her hand to her father, and he grasped it. With this show of willingness, the doctor rushed forward and supported his other hand and elbow. Her mother hurried to his side and supported the hand and arm she held.

'You're doing great, Yaseen. We are so proud of you.'

He looked up and smiled at his wife. The three of them helped him into the boot-like support that lay before the two banisters. The physiotherapist's room had been entirely set up to support this one treatment for her father.

Mohammed stood at the end of the two banisters, holding them both tightly, awaiting his father who stood at the opposite side. The doctor secured both of his feet into the support contraption, which looked like a pair of space boots in her eyes. This made her chuckle.

'You look like a spaceman, baba.'

'I don't feel like one, Ghaithaa.' He stifled a chuckle back as he clung to the arms of his wife and doctor.

She positioned herself in the middle of the two wooden banisters, in front of Mohammed. She watched as her mother and the doctor made a fuss. Her mother brushed the hair out of her father's eyes, and straightened the hem of his jeans so they didn't interrupt the aid of the space boots. The doctor was trying to straighten his back, moving his shoulders and adjusting the weight he was putting on each leg by pulling him this way and that.

'Yaseen, we've done this part many, many times before. Remember to try to even your balance. In your mind, think of how you should be standing before you try to walk. Legs apart, a shoulder's width, that's great, see you're doing so well already. Now remember, shoulders back, posture to the sky, that's brilliant. See, you can do it, we all know you can. Now. try to move your hands from the support of my arm and Nisreen's arm, that's good, now take hold of the banisters. Steady yourself, that's brilliant!'

She felt her chest inflate as she gasped, the image of her father standing tall and proud again. It was phenomenal beyond compare.

'Yaseen. Focus now on this next part. You're making great progress. Just – '

The doctor stopped and let his jaw fall.

She watched as her father slowly lifted his foot and his space man boot, and let it fall in front of him. His body faltered a little, but her mother caught his arm and pulled him back up. He moved his right foot in response, and it did the same, falling obediently next to the other boot.

She felt her skin tingle with excitement as she saw her father approach. He was smiling, and tall, taller than she'd ever seen him. He was smiling again, he was tall again, and he was walking again...

... Ghaithaa woke in a tent.

☙

Emad slept...

He sat at the table, a book before him. Out of the window, he could hear children playing ball in the street, and see the reflection of the setting sun on the glass. He looked down at the book in front of him. It was lined, with dates scribbled in the margins next to neatly curved handwriting.

He picked up a pen and began to start writing again. No sooner had his pen touched the paper, the doorbell rang, and he raised his head to listen for his mother's footsteps. She must be busy somewhere else in the house, he thought to himself, standing and tucking the chair under the table. He walked across the living room, his bare feet caressed by the patterned rug below, his eyes scanning the detailed paintings on the wall and framed family photographs. He smiled as he passed the pictures of his family on holiday, the pictures at celebrations and birthdays.

He continued into the hallway, a slightly darker part of the house with no windows, but lit up by the paintings hung on the wall, exhibited art crafted by him and his siblings. Butterflies, landscapes, families, he could explore for hours what he was thinking that day when he painted it, who he was thinking of, or where he was. Most of them had been painted at school, but he had been allowed to take some craft paper and paints home one day and that's when he painted the picture in the wooden frame for his mother and father. They had loved it. It was a painting of a lush green hill, tall trees, and a red picnic rug with them all sat on it. Often, a picture didn't come out the way he wanted it to in his head, but as soon as he looked at it he could remember.

'Emad, finish your savouries before you begin digging in on the sweets.' His mother patted his hand away from the box of cakes and pastries next to the bag they had carried the picnic in.

'Sorry, mama.' He slowly retracted his hand and let it settle on the other side of his bread. He was struggling to finish it. All he could think about was the creamy cakes in the box. All he could taste was sugar and cream.

'Emad!' His father scowled. He looked up at his father's face and smirked. He could hardly ever take him seriously when his face was so round and soft. Frustration and anger just didn't suit him.

His father tightened his brow.

'Sorry, baba.' He took a bite of his bread with a small smirk. His mother was smirking too. The two of them discussed the working week, whilst tucking in to more bread and hummus and vegetables.

He watched as their hands snatched away all of the food from in front of him. He'd had his eye on that roll, and that pepper, and that bowl of coriander hummus.

He let his bread slip into his left hand, whilst his right hand extended towards the cakes.

'I think I'll have a cake now, seeing as I've finished my savouries.' His father chortled, beating his hand to the box and grabbing the biggest of the cakes.

His face dropped and so did his bread.

'Please, baba! That's the best one! Mama, tell him!'

His mother began to laugh at the pair of them and took a bite into an apple, shaking her head.

'Maybe if you'd finished your bread, Emad...' His father teased, peeling the paper away from the bottom of the cake.

He could feel his eyes were desperate and his mouth was salivating.

His father opened his mouth and started to move the cake towards it.

'Mama!'

His father put the cake back down in the box and spluttered as he choked on a cough and a laugh.

His eyes seemed to disconnect from the picture, and his vision blurred a little. He had been staring too long. He wondered if there were cakes where his father was.

The doorbell rang once more, shrill and piercing.

He took a step closer and unlatched the lock and turned the handle.

'Hello, sweet tooth.' ...

... Emad woke in a tent.

☙

Majd slept...

...He steadied his balance on the wooden chair and attempted, once again, to follow the position of the hook on the back of the frame onto the nail in the wall. He exhaled as it finally slid into place. He stepped down from the chair and stood a step back to evaluate the painting. He nudged it slightly to the left a little, to steady its position on the wall. It looked good now. The painting was red with splashes of gold and blue, an abstract piece. The red colour was clearly painted with hard, fast strokes and a thick brush, whereas the blue and the gold were subtle and small and soft. The painting was a clashing of anger and peace, harmony and chaos. He smiled.

The painting stood out against the sparkling whiteness of the room. He turned to survey the four walls, all white, with blasts of colour from the paintings that adorned them. He liked to surround himself with colour. The floor was bright red.

He got back to putting hooks from a small box on the table onto the backs of frames.

'Excuse me, sir,' a voice behind him echoed. 'Is this gallery open?'

He turned and beamed at the visitor, a hunched old man in a grey jacket and yellow trousers.

'Why, yes, do come in!' He pulled out a chair from the central table for the old man, which was gratefully received and rested upon. 'I have to apologise, sir, we have only been open a day! So I'm still amidst putting up some of our artwork and canvases. But, please, do look around, and if you have any questions do ask.'

'I see, my son. A terrific place you have here. You'll be a popular gallery, I can tell!'

He smiled, this man seemed wise. He hoped this prophecy would be true. The artwork here was beautiful, and the building was too; a reconstructed library that had been destroyed in the conflict. The black iron spiralled staircase in the next room lead all the way to the fourth floor, where there remained some precious artwork from people he still knew, that he'd shared a camp with.

'Where would you recommend I start?' The old man's voice crackled like a piece of paper being crumpled in the palm of a hand.

'If you can get there, the fourth floor.' He smiled, helping the man stand up from the chair. 'I can lead the way if you'd like?'

The old man nodded, and for a while, he was fixated on the sparkle in his deep set, greying eyes.

He linked the man's arm in his own and lead him to the spiral staircase. Slowly they ascended, one foot in front of the other. The old man's wrinkled boots clunked against the stiff iron of the steps, and the sound echoed across the gallery. His own shoes squeaked in response. Their shoe conversation continued until they reached the top of the stairs.

The old man's chest heaved, and he collapsed in a conveniently placed armchair. 'Are you ok, sir?' He asked.

'I'll be fine, my son,' the old man chuckled. 'Just give me a second.'

After a while, he stood to his feet.

'Would you like me to tell you a bit about the paintings, sir?'

'Yes, please, that's very kind.' The old man held his hands behind his back and began to politely shuffle behind as he lead the way. They passed butterflies, doves, flowers, graveyards, families, guns, houses, cats.

'What tragic reminders of the conflict, eh?' The old man sighed.

'Yes, indeed, sir.'

'Do you know the artists?'

He smiled to himself.

'Yes, yes I do...'

...Majd woke in a tent.

∞

Nour slept...

...Her stomach felt tight. Her palms were sweaty holding onto her mother's hand. The sound of footsteps on stone and rubble was loud around her. She glanced over her shoulder. Behind her, seas of families, holding hands, were walking in the same direction. She looked ahead. The ground was dusty, covered with stones and rubble. It was being swept by people in high visibility jackets, and cleared with looming trucks. It was a vast, white, desert of rubble. Not a single building stood ahead. Just clouds of dust and groups of workers. She tightened her grip on her mother's hand.

They stood together. She looked up at the timber frame before her and half smiled. There were five workers in the same high visibility jackets as before climbing the timber frame like monkeys, cementing bricks, laying floors, preparing new glass.

'It looks wonderful, doesn't it, Nour?' Her mother squeezed her hand a little tighter.

'It looks like hope.'

'Sorry?'

'It looks like home.'

'What can we do to help?' Her father called up at the workers. One of them turned to look at them, climbed down the metal scaffolding, jumped to the dusty floor with a thud, and approached them. He shook all of their hands, one by one.

'You've been assigned to come here?' He asked, staring a while.

'Yes, this is our plot.' Her father answered, pulling a piece of printed paper out of his pocket and handing it to the man in the high visibility jacket.

'Very well, welcome home!' The man smiled, shaking her father's hand once again. Her father leaned across and gave her a kiss on the forehead.

'See, Nour. I told you it would all be ok, I told you we would come back.'

She beamed, catching the tear cascading down her cheek with the back of her palm.

'If you just put your belongings on the floor here, I'll have the team take them to your temporary accommodation. There are some new builds just down the road and you can stay there, it's like a little holiday for you, how does that sound?' He was looking right at her this time.

'That sounds great, thank you, sir.' She nodded. They followed his suggestion and took their bags off of their backs and put them in a collected heap on the floor. Three bags which carried all of their worldly possessions. Hers had a battered little zebra keying clipped onto it, a gift from her friend before they left the camp.

Sure enough, the workers came and labelled their bags with their names and new house number. They were taken away in a shiny white van.

She stood in the centre of the room. The smell of

polish and paint filled her nostrils and made her head feel dizzy and intoxicated. The sound of metal on tin rattled behind her. She turned to see her father using a knife to crack open another tin of paint.

'Would you like a hand, baba?' She walked over and crouched beside him, resting her hands on her already paint-splattered jeans.

'It's ok, just-needs-another-push...'

The lid of the can projected from the tin and landed face down on his jeans. He closed his eyes and laughed, throwing his head back.

'Oh dear, what's happened now?' Her mother's voice echoed from the doorway.

'Look at baba's jeans!' She exclaimed over her father's laughter.

'They're in fashion at the moment.' Her mother giggled with a wink. 'I'm just bringing in the last of the boxes now. The new furniture is so nice, Nour.'

'I'm glad. I'll come down in a minute, I'll just help baba paint the rest of my room.'

Her mother smiled and could be heard walking back down the new wooden stairs.

Her father lifted the lid of the paint tin off of his jeans, revealing a big purple circle, which made them roar with laughter again. He handed her a thick, bristled paint brush, and they dipped their brushes into the paint pot at the same time.

'Now, Nour, remember to wipe your paintbrush on the side of the tin to catch the excess before you put it onto the wall. We don't want any on the new floors.'

She nodded, obediently wiping the paintbrush

Every Child has the Right to Dream

against the sides of the tin, cupping her hand underneath it and brushing it carefully against the white wall...

... Nour woke in a tent.

Molly Masters

An Exhibition

The charity From Syria with Love runs touring exhibitions of the drawings of children in the Al Abrar camp in Lebanon. These are sold to raise funds for the camp and to help build a greater understanding of the lives of refugees.

The Purple Cat
Bayan

'I have drawn this picture because I like cats, I like nature, and especially the green colours in nature.'

Honey Bear
Douha

'I knew that the first drawings of cartoons and movement I created would be about a bear who wanted to have honey, and he was playing with the bees, and they started attacking him, and he couldn't find anywhere to run except for the sea so he jumped in the sea.'

The Alphabet Tree
Aya

'I have drawn a tree because my mum wanted me to draw a tree. So, I tried to represent my mum as a tree and my sisters are the branches which grow the fruit from the tree.'

Alan Kurdi
Douha

'I tried to show that everyone ignored the children in Syria who were killed through burning, weapons, torturing, and killing. The media only focused on Alan Kurdi who drowned.'

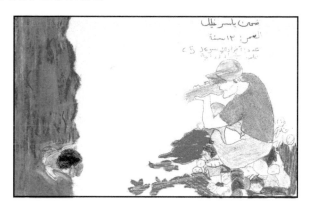

Alan Kurdi
Majd Krayem

Graveyard
Kawthar

Please...
Abdullah

'I drew this drawing on behalf of me, and my family.'

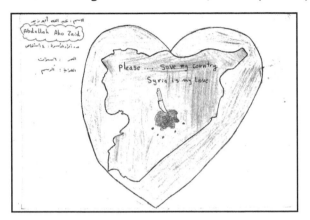

Warm Hearts
Aya

'I wish that the hearts of everyone in the world were connected to each other with love and peace.'

Family
Nada

The Arabic writing in the yellow coloured heart reads: 'Father and mother', the blue heart reads: 'Me', the red: 'My sister'. and in pink: 'My sister' again.

A Bloodied Rose
Roaa

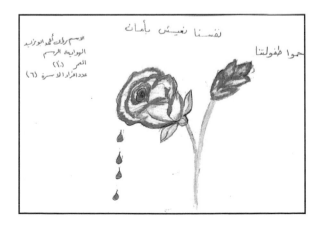

Tears
Tasneem

The Arabic writing reads: 'Hey eyes, don't cry.'

Art Class
Douha

Save the Children
Abdulrahman

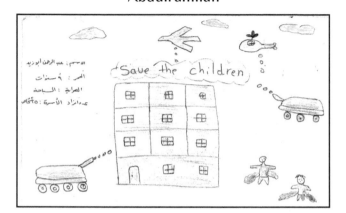

Cleansing Syria
Kawthar

Kawthar: 'My picture talks about the war in Syria and how the only people who are playing a part in the war are children and they are the ones trying to wipe the blood out of the country.' (*The Arabic writing reads: 'We have God and just God.'*)

At the Border
Douha

Doves
Kawthar

Pen Pals

Ghaithaa and Poppy are both ten year old girls. Ghaithaa is living in the Al Abrar displacement camp in Lebanon, and Poppy is living in England. They are pen pals. This first letter was written by Poppy after visiting the exhibition.

Hello!

My name's Poppy and I've always wanted a pen pal. After I saw the exhibition From Syria with Love, I really wanted to be in contact with one of the children in the refugee camp to hear their feelings. I enjoy anything to do with space. I also love music and I play the violin and I like writing poems. On the card that I made you, I also put a poem on that. I can't wait to have a pen pal!

Love from Poppy

Hi Poppy,

My name is Ghaithaa

I am really happy to talk with you.
   In this week we have Al Adha Eid, it is something we celebrate with our families and exchange congratulations in, so I wish a happy life to you.
   I like drawing and I am really interested to start to learn English. You seem very kind and sweet in the photo.
   Here is my photo:

Peace in Syria

Dear Gaithaa,

I am delighted to write to you. I wish you a happy Eid. I think you look very kind and sweet aswell. I also like drawing, especially trees and other nature. My name is a red flower in English. I have drawn some poppies around the page. What does your name mean? I have also drawn some doves for peace in Syria. I am glad you want to learn my language (English). Could you teach me hello and goodbye in arabic please. Again I'll say how glad I am to write to you and I think we have a lot in common.

All my love
From poppy
xx

Syria

Dear Poppy

I am sorry for being late.
The school started this week, also I usually go with auntie Rodeh to training centre.
I really liked your name meaning, I think my name means rain, but let me check and tell you later :)
You can't imagine how much happy I am because I am writing to you and I got a friend who likes drawing.
I hope to see more paintings from you...
The last paintings by me I sent it to Auntie Rodeh in order to share it in the new exhibition.
Finally İ will write the Arabic Meanings:
Hello is 'marhaba'.
Goodbye is 'wadaan' or 'bye'.
In next time I will write to you what did I learn in English.

Your friend Ghaithaa

Dear Gaithaa,

I am nearly happy to be writing to you too. Me and my family will definately visit the exhibition and I can't wait to see your picture. When we go I will buy the picture and hang it on my wall. On a seperate peice of paper I will draw a picture of me and you holding hands and I hope you like it. I am glad you have started school and hope you like it there. Thank you for the translations and If there are any words you would like to learn in English, I can send them to you. I wish you and your family the best of luck.

your friend Poppy
xxx

'How do you feel today?'

I feel only five years old, because these five years of war have taught me the cruelty of war.

I feel as if I am an old child. I'm not sure what an old child is, I just feel that way.

I feel happy because I'm singing in a band now, and I feel I am myself when I sing.

I feel I'm starting to like the tents more now, because the war in Syria is going to last longer, I can feel it.

I feel I want to thank Auntie Um Nour for making the children so happy.

I feel confused and frustrated, we have been forbidden so many of our rights in these five years.

I feel we have grown old before we've grown up, and we think too much.

I feel that every time I think I'm starting to get used to the tents, I'm not.

Douha's Diary ll

As always, my mum woke me to get ready for the art centre. My mum insists on taking me with her just to feel more comfortable. At 09:00 am we took a bus and I was very sleepy. Shortly, we arrived and there was a small surprise: it was a day off in the art centre! At 10:00 am, I got back to my mum's work centre, and she was shocked, of course. I don't like the centre where she works so I stayed until 12:00 pm and I was really bored, so I went to a break room and told my mum that I will sleep. Suddenly my mum was saying: "wake up the day is finished".

We arrived home and my mum had a headache, I went directly to the kitchen and started to drink water.

After sunset we started to make dinner it was grilled chicken, because my mum was tired and she couldn't cook for us, after that I went to the pharmacy to buy some painkillers for her, even after she took it she was tired. In order to make all of these moments valuable, Ahmad, my nephew, started to cry loudly. So everyone slept early and I couldn't watch my Indian movie.

Thursday was very busy. As always waking up early, but this time my mother's kindness made me wake up at 10:00 am to register in the school. To be a student here is very, very expensive. I used to be with Aya and Tasneem in the same school, but this year I couldn't find a place in their school. There is a private school here (Omar Al Mokhtar), but to register there I need to pay more than $3000 per year.

What İ want to say that because all of these and the expensive education, my mother talked with her friend who is Lebanese, and this friend made an application in order to make me attend in an educational institute, and it was a golden chance to me. They accepted me and in the next few days I will start to attend there. On this Thursday, I went with my mom to do the approval for the institute, and after that I asked my mom if I could go to my old school to see my friends, because I am free for a few days and they have exams. When I got back to home, instead of seeing some kind of good, my sister Kawthar had left the dish washing to me, she said it was my turn. I hate dish washing so I washed some glasses and then I said I have a stomach ache, and guess what? They shouted at me and I had to continue the washing.

From time to time I spend a day with the children and try to teach them an English song, and if they can sing it after practicing, my mom lets them sing it at an upcoming party. On Thursday they came, but my mom didn't allow us to practice because of her headache, and my nephew.

Actually I felt shy a little bit but I didn't show that, so I went to the children and said: "go now we will meet sometime later". We have had this meeting every week for two years here and no one can handle our loud voices, but I thought about my mum and how much patient she is, especially since she went to the next city and sent the paintings then came back here. She does a lot for us. After while the neighbours started to come and congratulate my sister on my nephew, and that meant me and Kawthar had to make coffee. I started and made a bad coffee, obviously they didn't like it, and they asked Kawthar to make it. Mother was there and she understood what I did, so she shouted a little bit at me, I felt bad and went to sleep. Then I saw my favourite movie on TV and I changed my mind and took some money to buy nuts and Pepsi. Then I called Bayan and Aya, and told them to set glasses and some dishes. We watched the movie, and after that I had to wash the dishes it was my turn again. My mom suddenly said: "What happened? Did you take your decision to put the cover on your head?" I said we will talk later and I went to sleep. The day finally finished.

Special Delivery

There was food.
There were boxes.
There was a van.
And there was Bayan.

The sound of the engine died. Its rattling whirrs became slower and steadier, and its jittering suspension staggered and stopped with a jolt. Bayan's head bobbed with the impact.

'Here we are!' Uncle Ali declared. 'Let's hop out.'

Bayan unclipped her belt with her small fingers and slid from the leather seat of the van out into the noisy, open street. Horns beeped and the bells of bicycles rang, the music of busy life. She didn't hear this often.

Uncle Ali was already walking ahead, towards the open double doors of the building. She followed after him with light, cub-like prances, hopping onto the pavement and into the building. Through the glass she could already see people busying inside. People bent over boxes, taped up tight and bulging to the brim, picking them up and squeezing through the throng to take them outside.

'Are you ok to get stuck in then, Bayan?' Uncle Ali said, kneeling at her side.

'Yes, thank you, Uncle Ali.' Bayan smiled in response.

He left her side and hurried to where the adults were busy with papers attached to clipboards. Bayan looked around for a clearing amongst the chaos. She dashed for a smaller box, more suited to her size, and picked it up with both of her arms around it's middle.

She lifted it up to the height of her knees before it came crashing down to the floor again.

'Bayan, like this.' Her friend Kawthar instructed, showing how to hook her hands underneath the box instead of around it. Bayan nodded and did the same, now able to lift the box higher and scoot out of the door with lots of little steps at a time. This time she approached a nearby car with an open boot instead of the white van she and Uncle Ali had arrived in. A man stood receiving the boxes from the children and taking a tally.

'Well done, Bayan, good work!' He exclaimed, taking the weight of the box from her small arms.

'It's good to help out!' She smiled. 'Where are we taking these food boxes today?'

'Most of them will be going to the Tal Wazi refugee camps, Bayan, and some to other families on our lists elsewhere. I'm packing this car for Tal Wazi, and there should be 35 aid boxes to give to 35 tents.'

'The families are going to be so excited.' Bayan said gleefully, knowing the feeling all too well.

When she re-entered the room, Bayan saw Kawthar making a video with Auntie Rodeh. She was standing confidently, smiling and speaking very clearly. She had taken off her sunglasses and positioned them neatly on top of her black hijab. She was wearing the purple t-shirt Bayan had been admiring for weeks. She wished that she could be like Kawthar.

Kawthar gave the same facts about the 35 aid boxes and the 35 tents, and explained that the film was going to be sent back to From Syria With Love in England to post online. That way, people who had donated money could see how their support was having a direct impact, that's what Auntie Rodeh said. A mass of people scurried around and shouted, carrying the weight of their boxes on their fronts as they hunched and hurried out of the door. The boxes were heavy with food. In the corner, Douha and Mousa stood checking over some of the last few to be packed.

'Can I help? Can I help?' Bayan tapped on Mousa's arm and Douha's back. They turned in unison and laughed.

'Of course, Bayan.' Douha smiled. 'Come on in!'

Bayan moved onto the other side of the box that they were packing, opposite them so that she could see their work and faces. Mousa was ticking items off on a sheet (he knew how to write) and Douha was packing items into the box and squishing the contents down until the box was fuller than full. The packets crinkled as they were handled and squished and packed, and Bayan watched with rounded eyes as the gold and silver of the precious packages were lifted and placed into the box. Bottles of oil and water, cooking sauces, pasta, dried food, cans; each box was brimming with the things they had missed for so long, brimming with items packed by loving hands, large and small. Bayan smiled inside knowing that the families and children, the same as her, the same as Douha, the same as Mousa, the same as Kawthar, the same as Auntie Rodeh, the same as Uncle Ali, and the same as the man at the car, were all going to receive today the food that was so special and so much missed. She remembered how exciting their first boxes were, and the many smiles, applauses and cheers they still brought, years on.

There was food.
There were boxes.
There was a car
And there was Douha.

Douha watched the remaining boxes as they convoyed their way to the van and the car. It was a procession of eyes peeping over the tops of boxes, each person behind almost unrecognisable. Inside, she heard Bayan groan jokingly under the weight of one of the final boxes, twice her size. Mousa struggled with another, and she rushed to help him as he launched it from his thigh to his shoulder. They laughed together and she followed behind him with her hands pressed up against the back of the box to make sure it didn't slip.

Douha stood back again as she watched Uncle Ali stack the boxes high into the van, and pass them to the man next to the car. She watched as the cars passed the parking area at speed. She breathed in the air of exhaust fumes and cloud. The air tasted different here.

'Right! All done!' Uncle Ali jumped from the open sliding door of the van and onto the concrete. He toppled a little and the children below all extended their arms to cushion him. It made him chuckle.

'So, who would like to come with me in the car this week, then, eh?'

Many a small hand shot up and waved, and Uncle Ali was swamped around his torso with arms and flailing limbs. Douha had her hand high in the air, but was possibly too far away for him to see.

'Me! Me! Me! Me!' The children chanted like tweeting birds.

'Enough, enough, my children!' He chortled, using his arms to gesture and hush their noise. 'How about you, Douha? You haven't come with me in a while.'

A few dissatisfied groans came from the tweeting birds.

Douha's face lit up and she made her way over to the passenger side of the car whilst Uncle Ali fumbled in his pocket for the keys.

'The rest of you, all bundle into the van, please! And wait for Auntie Rodeh!'

Douha heard the click of the car keys and opened the passenger door. Uncle Ali bumped his head as he crouched to get in and Douha giggled.

'Are we going to Tal Wazi, Uncle Ali?' She asked.

'Yes, my child. We are going to deliver the 35 families their boxes,' He turned as he heard one of the back doors open and someone get in. 'This is my friend, he has come to help us and has been asked to take a video of our journey for From Syria With Love, would you like to be in it?'

Douha nodded frantically with a beaming smile.

Uncle Ali started up the engine and a loud, upbeat Arabic song began to play through the stereo. The music made her sing, she missed singing to music in the camp.

'Ready to film, Douha?' the man in the back asked, as Uncle Ali turned onto the busy road.

'Yes!' She turned around from the front seat to face the camera on his smartphone.

He mimed a count down on his fingers and she began to speak:

'I would like to thank Uncle Ali a lot because he always takes and accompanies us on our From Syria With Love journeys and distributions,' she turned to Uncle Ali. 'And soon he will teach us driving!'

Uncle Ali laughed from his belly, a deep and rumbling laughter, and he shook his head whilst smiling.

Douha and Aya.

Auntie Rodeh

Rodeh is both a mother in the camp, and the person responsible for From Syria With Love's work in Lebanon.

She is like our best friend firstly, then our mother. Her open arms warm us and her affection glows like a yellowing sunrise.

She is like the mother of the whole camp.

She is like a smile, I feel happy every time I see her.

She is like a looking glass, I cry when I think about it. She is supporting us all and we can see our future so clearly and beautifully with her, in her loving words and her encouraging embrace.

She is like Syria. She looks like Syria. She has a big heart just like Syria.

She is like my grandmother, she always gives us a delicious snack and food made with love.

She is like my mother in looks. When we see her we feel warm, she looks familiar, like family; a mother, a grandmother, a sister, a cousin, an auntie all in one.

She is like a rock, she looks so strong.

She is like spring. She brings new life, new hope in her words.

She is what joy looks like.

She is like a teacher, a voice of motivation. We love when she shows us the photos of the exhibitions in England and tells us how we are helping people by drawing. We love when she tells us to keep going, to continue our education.

She is like an open book, teaching us what life is, how to overcome hard times, how to be charitable, not to give up, how to be strong, how to be patient, how to draw, how to help people modestly and kindly.

Auntie Rodeh tells us, 'You will build Syria again, be strong.'

Auntie Rodeh taught us sometimes a tent may be more important and more beautiful than a castle.

'What makes you...?'

Q: What makes you happy?

Nada: When I am told there is a party.

Nour: When I pass my classes at school.

Bayan: When I sing about Syria.

Majd: When an exhibition is successful.

Ghaithaa: When my father is healed.

Mohammed: When my parents are satisfied about me.

Q: What makes you feel strong?

All: When we have parties and know that we are helping people through our drawings.

Q: Where do you see yourselves in ten years time?

All: 'Syria!'

Apart from Mousa, he laughed and said: 'I will be engaged by then!'

Q: What inspires you?

Nada, Majd, Ghaithaa: The parties we have had.

Bayan: When I participate in distributing aid baskets.

Mousa, Mohammed: Our parents.

Pictures of Eid

The colours dance, and the children do too.

The reds and yellows and blues and greens are filled with air and attached to long strings, and they hang in between each tent like miniature rainbows. On this day, the vibrancies stand out more than the dust underfoot and the yellowing white of the tents. The camera's lens captures the colours swaying in the gentle breeze along with the music; it follows quickly as little children run laughing underneath them and into the hubbub of the party.

It turns and zooms on groups of children posing and giggling against a makeshift backdrop of white sheets draped over a washing line with balloons attached. The children bustle and squeal as they dig deep into a cardboard box. They take out hats, feather boas, deely boppers and masks; pull them over their heads and race back into the eye of the other cameras. Parents smile proudly behind their mobile phones, shouting countdowns at the children and laughing as the flash explodes and many of them blink.

The camera turns once more and follows two excited girls as they run to join the back of a very long queue. At the front of it, a small boy sits on a plastic chair in front of a woman with a thick paintbrush and palette of soft paints in bold colours. She cups his face with her left hand and paints a crimson heart on his cheek with the other. The brush strokes are rounded and delicate, despite the boy's excited wriggles. As he pushes himself up from his seat, and thanks the lady for his face paint, another smaller boy squirms his way to the front of the queue and into the seat. The rest of the children shout in protest, and the boy is ushered to the back of the line, sulking a little. Upon arriving at the back of the queue, the boy notices the camera overseeing the action and begins to jump, smile and wave in its direction. The camera pursues more waves, and as it moves around the square, it receives many a greeting and an excited wave from children, mothers and fathers. The parents are mainly sitting at chairs basking in the sun and inside open tents, watching their little ones race around and enjoy the celebration. They wave politely at the camera as it passes.

There is a man sat on a stool next to the wall, where a speaker balances and sings out gentle Arabic melodies to which many sing along. A small girl balances on his lap and appears to help him choose the songs from his mobile phone. The music brings everyone together in the centre of the party square. The children dance in large circles, some holding their mother's hands and spinning, others dance alone with their arms above their heads, chanting along. A boy sits atop the shoulders of a volunteer at the camp. He squeals in delight as the volunteer takes both of his hands and holds them out to his sides. He mimics the sounds of a plane engine as he spins around, the boy's arms like propellers. The song finishes and the dancers and singers remain where they are and applaud and laugh, cheering themselves, the idols of their own concert. As the next one begins, a woman comes to the centre of the circle with a microphone. The children clap in time and she sings to an Arabic song; the microphone is passed around through all of the small hands, met by small voices, singing along to the song one by one. Some children smirk and sing quietly, holding onto their mother's hand. Some children laugh and barely sing at all. Some children sing very loudly into the microphone. The smiling and clapping continues.

The camera spins around and watches four boys sitting on top of the brick wall, swinging their legs and watching everybody below like perching birds on a telephone wire. Their mothers call up at them from the ground, telling them to be careful. Below the wall, a taller, older girl attempts to control a bubbly crowd of children as they jump at her heels. In her left hand she holds a silver can of glitter spray, and teases them a little by squirting it every so often, releasing a trail of stars whooshing above their heads. They scream and laugh in delight and try to catch the spray on their heads, in their hair, on their clothes, and in their hands. The older girl smiles and shakes the can again. The children come running back. She holds down the nozzle and an entire shower of stars fall over the children and they are almost too busy running and bumping into each other and catching the glitter to make a sound. Their smiles speak for them. A voice of a woman speaks from behind the camera's eye, she seems to say something about the now glittery silver shirt of one boy and he shakes his head and laughs, small tears running from his cheeks after giggling so hard.

The camera takes a panoramic view of the party. A small girl with her curly black hair in pigtails stands on top of a chair with the microphone to her mouth. She smiles and sings a celebration song, her mother supporting the back of the chair and patting her back. Everyone cheers for her. Another girl comes into the shot, wearing a bright yellow t-shirt and a matching canary coloured hijab. She wears a camera around her own neck, and pouts for the camera as it pans past her. At the centre of the party, mothers lead their children into a large circle of holding hands, and they walk around chanting and singing, the small children looking up and following what their mothers and older siblings do.

The children dance, and the colours do too.

This was inspired by the pictures and videos of the Eid celebrations in the camp. They were sent to From Syria With Love as a thank you.

A Message From...

Nour
12 years old

At first I didn't know where we are going, when we will go back, what is going on, why this happened to us? Now I know one thing: I am very happy while I am writing this and I am imagining how it will be published and so many people will read it: just don't give up.

Bayan
11 years old

I don't know what to say. Actually I just know these words and I want everyone to know it. My mum always says Syria may get weaker but it will never die.

Majd
12 years old

I think it is our destiny, my parents immigrated to Syria from Palestine before, and now it is my turn.

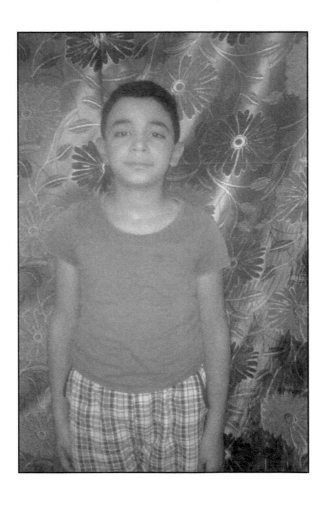

Mohammed
12 years old

I always wanted to be a doctor, but now I must be a doctor to treat my father. When I think about home, I just see my grandfather's house, and I miss it a lot. I always pray to Syria and to get back to Syria.

Nada
10 years old

I always think tomorrow it will be better I am sure. Everything will be good, I promise. We will draw and draw we must help the people.

Ghaithaa
10 years old

I love my mother. When I feel bad or when I feel good I read the Quran, it makes me feel better always. I love auntie Rodeh also, she is my best friend. I always pray and dream that my father will walk again someday.

Douha, Aya and Tasneem
14 and 15 years old

In school they named us the Funny Triplets. We always sit, talk, and dream about our music band. We haven't made it yet but we will. Douha will play guitar, Aya will play piano and Tasneem will play Nay. Also we dream to make our own exhibition we dream about success.

Kawthar
17 years old

I have many things to say, but the conclusion is: I would like to thank my mother, Baraa, Hala, and Molly, because they gave me the chance to talk and to express my feelings. In this book there is a paragraph talking about me. I want to say that I will keep going to the end, and don't forget that failure is the first step to success.

Auntie Rodeh

If you allow me, I want to share this: My dream started from an exhibition in the camp and suddenly it moved to exhibitions in UK. I saw the children when they cried from happiness, but let me say this: If Baraa wasn't here for us, we wouldn't make it. He is the one who listens to me and understands my ideas. I want to thank him and thank you all.

Strength and Forgiveness

Douha: I am strong but I cannot forgive people because they are cowards, but I am strong like my mother.

Tasneem: I am strong because I am learning and I will learn until the end, but I cannot forgive.

Ghaithaa: Every time I read the Quran I feel strong, and I forgive because God forgives.

Kawthar: I became strong after my divorce and sometimes I can forgive.

Mohammed: I am strong because my father is disabled and I must take his role, and I forgive because God forgives.

Bayan: I am strong because of the war. I can't forgive anyone who forced us to leave our homeland.

Mousa: I don't know, but I can't let anyone feel sad.

Majd: After all we have passed through, I became strong, and I can forgive everyone because I have a pure heart.

The UK Contributors

Kathryn Aldridge-Morris is a writer of short stories and flash fiction. She also specialises in writing materials to help refugees and asylum seekers learn English.

Nikita Austen is a graphic designer and artist who runs an Etsy shop and Facebook page under the name of 'Buddy's Little Daisy'.

Brian Bilston is typically described as the 'Poet Laureate of Twitter'. He won the 2015 Great British Write Off poetry prize, and his first collection of poetry 'You Caught the Last Bus Home' was published on October 2016.

Gillian Cross best known for her series 'The Demon Headmaster', which was later turned into a TV series by the BBC. She is also the winner of the 1990 Carneige Model and the 1992 Whitbread Children's Book Award.

Poppy Frutos-Morris is a ten-year-old school girl who is passionate about helping refugees. After she visited the FSWL exhibition, she organised a clothes collection for the refugees in Calais.

Molly Masters is a volunteer at From Syria With Love, and a student of English Literature. She is 19 years old, and entering her second year at university.

Caroline Moorehead is a writer and human rights journalist. She is a governor of the British Institute of Human Rights and was appointed an OBE in 2005 for services to literature.

The Charity

From Syria With Love acts as a bridge between refugees and the British public. It ws founded by Syrian, Baraa Ehssan Kouja and tours the UK exhibiting the artwork of Syrian children, including those you have read about in this book. The art is also available for sale, and this raises money that goes directly to help children in refugee camps across Lebanon and Syria where there is a lack of healthcare, education and sanitation, to ensure that their lives are as comfortable and safe as possible. The art also makes a unique connection between individual refugees and people in Britain, and our shared humanity, and so helps build integration and understanding.

You can make a donation or follow the charity's work at our website (fromsyriawithlove.com) and on Facebook, YouTube, Twitter (@FromSyriaWL) and Instagram (@fromsyriawl). From Syria With Love take no management fees or administration costs.

If you would like to help set up an exhibition near you, or support the charity's work in any other way, please contact: info@fromsyriawithlove.com. For information about the book, please contact: author@fromsyriawithlove.com